D0507880

Practical Know-how in the Wardrobe

SIMON &
SCHUSTER

LONDON • NEW YORK • SYDNEY • TORONTO

First published in Great Britain by
Simon & Schuster UK Ltd 2007
A CBS Company

Copyright © this compilation WI Enterprises Ltd, 2007
All rights reserved.
Illustrations copyright © Jane Norman 2007

ISBN 1 8473 7007 1
EAN 978 1 8473 7007 5

Simon and Schuster UK Ltd

Africa House
64–78 Kingsway
London WC2B 6AH

This book is copyright under the Berne Convention.
No reproduction without permission.
All right reserved.

1 3 5 7 9 10 8 6 4 2

Design and illustrations by Jane Norman
Text by Vicky Pepys and Jenny Kieldsen
Jacket design by Kari Brownlie
Printed and bound in China

Contents

Introduction

Does your heart sink when you open the
wardrobe door? Are your clothes crammed in so
tightly that you've no idea what's inside. If this
scenario sounds familiar, it's time for some
serious sorting out and this little book is full of
useful tips to help you to do it. You'll find
valuable advice on choosing the right
accessories: footwear, handbags, jewellery,
even underwear, are important to
the overall look.
And once you know how to care for and store
your clothes, shoes and accessories — and how
to deal with any emergencies – you'll be
able to enjoy them all year round.

" *Create your own visual style...*
let it be unique for yourself and yet
identifiable for others. **"**

Orson Welles, 1915–1985

Your Wardrobe

Create your own space

If you can, sacrifice some house or room space to create a dedicated dressing area – well lit with a full-length mirror, iron and ironing board to hand. In this environment you can easily find what you're looking for and make sure you're looking good from all angles.

Keep your wardrobe smelling fresh

Put only clean clothes in the wardrobe; a worn
garment will contaminate everything else.

Never return laundered clothes to the wardrobe
unless they are bone dry.

Hook lavender bags or cedar wood rings over
coat hangers for good smells and to
deter moths.

" It is fancy rather than taste which produces so many new fashions. "

Voltaire, 1694–1778

" Fashion is the science of appearance, and it inspires one with the desire to seem rather than to be."

Henry Fielding, 1701–1754

Sorting clothes

Do a sort-out every season; but don't lose
yourself in the process. First and foremost
decide who and what you want to be this
season; it's a good opportunity for a
change of image.

❝ Clothes and manners do not make the man; but, when he is made, they greatly improve his appearance. ❞

Henry Ward Beecher, 1813–1887

Make sure you can see it

If your wardrobe rail is at shoulder height,
consider re-fixing it at chest height so that
you can add a shelf above the rail. Shoes and
handbags stored at eye level become much
easier to find and save you scrabbling
about under the rail.

Hang on!

Discard all wire hangers (keep one for removing static), return all flimsy plastic dry cleaning hangers and replace with substantial padded hangers or 'curved shoulder' wooden or plastic ones. Straight hangers make indentation marks on shoulders.

Your Wardrobe

Store it away

Pack up and 'bag' the bulk of pales and thin cottons or linens at the beginning of autumn so you'll have more space in your wardrobe for your winter styles; the same goes for Spring. Remember to flat pack woollens so they're not distorted on a hanger.

“*Don't spend two dollars to dry clean a shirt. Donate it to the Salvation Army instead. They'll clean it and put it on a hanger. Next morning buy it back for seventy-five cents.*”

Anon.

Be ruthless

Try on every single item of clothing once a
season. If it's too big, throw it away; big
clothes simply make you look bigger. If it's too
small by a couple of sizes, keep it in case you
lose some weight. If it's too small by more than
three sizes, or you haven't worn it for three
years, chuck it out. If it's in good nick,
take it to the charity shop.

So, so special

Some outfits are just too special to throw away, but they take up valuable rail space. If you think they have a social history or historical fashion value, pass them on to the local applied arts museum, theatre wardrobe department or university fashion design course. Someone will love them as much as you do.

Your Wardrobe

" *Fashions fade, style is eternal.* **"**

Yves Saint Laurent, b. 1940

❝ *You are never fully dressed until you wear a smile.* **❞**

Anon

What to Wear

Timeless advice

Classic styles are always a better fashion
option than up-to-the-minute trendy styles,
which may look dated next season. Make your
classics trendy with inexpensive jewellery
or accessories.

A core item

A dark tailored suit is essential for business and formal occasions. Yet a suit isn't necessarily a fitted jacket; a shirt style, blouson or safari style can look equally smart. Look further down the rail for alternative styles in the same fabrics and create your own smart suit.

What to Wear

❝It is the awkward man, whose evening dress does not fit him, whose gloves will not go on, whose compliments will not come off...❞

G.K Chesterton, 1874–1936

How many of each?

Tops require more laundering, therefore try to have two for every one 'bottom'. A good basis is 2 jackets, 3 bottoms, 5 tops; this should get you through the week.

Essential white shirt

A good buy every season is a white cotton shirt. Classic semi-tailored styles, the best you can afford, will work for both smart and casual. White cotton, however carefully cared for, often loses its freshness and its bright whiteness and really only looks good when it's relatively brand new.

Little Black Dress

The LBD is a staple garment for the party season. Choose a long or cocktail length sleeve if your don't like your arms and, if you choose a sleeveless style, make sure bra straps are not visible. Wear with a glitzy wrap or pashmina.

What to Wear

> 66 *Style is the dress of thought; a modest*
> *dress, Neat, but not gaudy,*
> *will true critics please.* 99
>
> Samuel Wesley, 1766–1837

Patterns and prints

Patterns and prints work better on tops than on bottoms. They add interest to an otherwise plain outfit. The general rule is that big prints look better on larger frames and tiny ones on smaller frames...but all prints, even spots or stripes, can date quickly.

" *Every generation laughs at the old fashions, but follows religiously the new.* **"**

Henry David Thoreau, 1817–1862

Ready to wear

Every evening, hang clothes that don't need laundering on a hanger to air before putting them away. Even better, iron or mist a heavily creased garment and check for loose threads, loose buttons, falling hems etc. Then you'll know it's ready to wear next time. The same goes for shoes and boots – a quick wipe or polish before putting them back will save time later.

" *Fashions, after all, are only induced epidemics.* "

George Bernard Shaw 1866–1950

How to wear V-necks

A very deep V-neck is designed to be worn with a t-shirt or camisole top, but a simple 'V' of lace, carefully sewn into the *décolleté*, makes it less revealing and, without the layers, a little cooler.

Layers

Don't rely on the weather forecast; as seasons change it's easy to be too hot or too cool all on the same day. Learn to layer. Thin layers of jersey separates (camisole, t-shirt, wrap top) look fashionable in coordinating, classic or bold colours, and can be peeled off as the day warms up.

Choosing the right size

The critical measurements for clothing are:
bust, waist, hips, and length. These
measurements will help you to find the right
size within fashion size ranges and to
get a good fit.

Size 16

Forty per cent of the UK population is a size 16 and over. If you fit into this category, try to avoid elasticated leggings, tracksuit bottoms and trousers. The elastic cuts into the tummy and the back, creating unnecessary bulges. It's better to wear flat-front styles without bulky pockets.

Special all-day events

Going to a wedding that's an all-day-into-evening event? Wear a suit with a change of tops, or a dress with a change of day and evening accessories. Prepare for a change in temperature and weather with wraps and shawls and take a change of shoes.

Going out straight after work?

Wear a classic pant or skirt with your day top
then switch to something a little more frivolous;
add evening jewellery, a deeper lipstick, a
higher heel, and away you go.

❋

❝ *You should never have your best trousers
on when you go out to fight for
freedom and truth.* **❞**

Henrik Ibsen, 1828–1906

37

"Laundry is the only thing that should be separated by colour."

Anon.

Washing and Ironing

Keep corduroy fluff-free

Turn cord garments inside out before putting in
the washing machine. This also works well if
you don't want denim and black jeans to fade.

Before you start washing

Check all pockets for money, tissues and small toys that can ruin a whole wash. Do up buttons and zip up zips. Check the label for laundry instructions.

To hand wash silk

Wash only if the label recommends it. Add a tablespoon of vinegar to the final rinse to give the garment a professional crispness.

" ** *I am well aware that an addiction to silk underwear does not necessarily imply that one's feet are dirty.* **"

Albert Camus, 1913-1960

Ties

After washing and ironing, put the tie on
a hanger to dry.

To remove stains from neckties

Slip a paper towel inside the tie to avoid wetting the reverse side. Using hot water, a disposable cloth and a little washing up liquid, dab the spot, letting the paper towel absorb any excess liquid. Use a hair dryer to dry the area as quickly as possible, to prevent a watermark forming and the tie from shrinking.

A clean tie attracts the soup of the day.

Anon.

To wash a baseball cap

Put the cap in the top rack of the dishwasher, if you have one, and run a normal cycle. Leave it to air dry on a flat surface so that it retains its shape.

Mildew stains

Mix salt and lemon juice, and rub well into the stained area before washing in the normal way.

To press velvet

Press on the reverse side: turn the fabric inside
out and cover with a damp cotton cloth
before ironing.

Shiny not nice...

Always use a damp or special ironing cloth to
iron collars and reveres on jackets; otherwise
the seams and corners will become shiny
with the heat.

Sharp collars

Always iron collars from the pointed tip to the
centre back so you're not left with
wrinkles in the corners.

✴

*❝Relax, Georgie, I'm just making my collar
and cuffs match.❞*

Carole Lombard, 1908–1942

Special protection

Use a specialist hosiery bag when washing tights and stockings in the washing machine (light cycle and maximum 30-40 degrees). These, unlike a normal washing bag, have a fully enclosed 'neck' making it impossible for buttons or zips from other garments to come into contact with delicates. Alternatively, put delicate items in an old pillowcase.

" First you forget names, then you forget faces. Next you forget to pull your zipper up and finally, you forget to pull it down."

George Burns

Caring for Clothes

Sticky zip

A piece of beeswax in your home sewing kit
(strengthens thread for sewing on buttons) will
lubricate the teeth of a zip, especially after dry
cleaning. A lead pencil 'drawn' up and
down the zip works too .

Mend before cleaning

If mending a hem, do so before washing or
going to the dry cleaners as the 'line', which
acts as a guide, may be lost during the
process. Also, mend broken stitches in seams,
armholes etc. as the break in stitching will
surely lengthen with laundering
or cleaning.

❝*What breaks in a moment may take years to mend.***❞**

Swedish proverb

Pleats will be pleased

Don't hang a pleated skirt on a hanger...the
'pull' on the sides will make the pleats go
squiffy; fold into a tube with pleats in order and
store in a stocking or a leg of an
old pair of tights.

❝ Fashion is born by small facts, trends, or even politics, never by trying to make little pleats and furbelows, by trinkets, by clothes easy to copy, or by the shortening or lengthening of a skirt. ❞

Elsa Schiaparelli, 1896–1973

" *I pity the man who wants a coat so cheap that the man or woman who produces the cloth will starve in the process.* **"**

Benjamin Harrison, 1835–1901

Dirty dust

Garment bags don't just protect against dust
but also creases…on the rail, but also in a
suitcase. If no flimsy plastic ones are
available try swing bin liners.

Be careful

Use fabric conditioner sparingly; it softens
fibres by breaking them down and prematurely
ageing them. Use only in hard water areas.

Repairing buttons

Some buttons may be damaged in the dry cleaning process. Get your sewing kit ready: thick fabrics need a shank fastening; with thin fabrics you need to sew the button closer to the surface of the fabric.

Caring for Clothes

" Day has put on his jacket, and around/
His burning bosom buttoned it with stars. "

Oliver Wendell Holmes, 1809–1894

Sticky purchase

Invest in a sticky roller for removing fluff, dandruff and cat and dog hair from garments as you put them away. Ordinary sticky tape works equally well wrapped the 'wrong' way round the hand…rubber gloves and a damp new dishcloth also work well.

Caring for Clothes

Fuzz free

Defuzzing tools are available to remove knit
'bobbles' from woollies, but a new disposable
razor used very lightly and carefully
works rather well too.

Brilliantly cleaned bags

Polish leather handbags regularly with furniture cream then store under cover, filled with paper to retain the shape. Plastic bags just need a wipe with a damp cloth and a bit of polish, while fabric and straw bags can be cleaned with the foam from whisked up detergent, which should be wiped off quickly.

Stains

Treat stains immediately; they are far easier to
remove than those that have been allowed to
dry. Most everyday stains can be removed by
washing or gently scrubbing the stained area
using a nailbrush and washing powder or
soaking first in a cold water solution.
Remember that hot water and ironing
sets a stain.

Velvet care

Velvet isn't easy to look after; it marks and loses its 'pile'. Store face-to-face, as in pile-to-pile, to retain the structure and always press it on the wrong side, again face-to-face, so it isn't squashed on to a hard surface.

Tips for packing

If you're packing a formal jacket, stuff socks
and pants into the shoulders so
they don't flatten.

✳

" *A razor can't be sharpened on a
piece of velvet.* **"**

Anon.

" It is the unseen, unforgettable, ultimate accessory of fashion that heralds your arrival and prolongs your departure."

Coco Chanel, 1883–1971

Accessorize

Ribbon, braid and lace

Don't be afraid to experiment with
embellishment. Interesting ribbon, braiding and
lace can create a completely new look for an
old outfit, particularly effective on skirts to add
interest to hemlines...and on collars and cuffs.

The right glasses

Trendy spectacles can change your look completely. It is always good to have a spare pair for your handbag or desk drawer. If your wardrobe is predominantly black and grey, go for monochrome, clear or silver frames. Cream, beige, sand, tan and chocolate work well with tortoiseshell and gold specs.

Accessorize

"*He saw nearly all things as through a glass eye, darkly.*"

Mark Twain, 1835–1910

Sunglasses

They add an air of style, even if they're not on
your face, but on top of your head. As a rule:
round faces need frames that are the same
width or slightly wider than the widest part of
the face; long faces need frames that are wider
than their depth; square faces need curves;
heart-shaped faces need detail at the bottom
to make the lower face look wider.

Accessorize

Style is a simple way of saying complicated things.

Jean Cocteau, 1889–1963

" *The first thing any comedian does on getting an unscheduled laugh is to verify the state of his buttons.* **"**

W.C Fields, 1880–1946

Buttons galore

Older vintage buttons, not necessarily antiques, are much more interesting then modern cheap plastic ones. Old-style buttons add interest to affordable clothing that has cost buttons in itself! If you're lucky, you'll have inherited grandma's button bag or box; if not, scour the charity shops and flea markets for unusual quality fastenings.

Look after your jewellery

Store beaded necklaces in boxes as they will get dusty if left out. For easy retrieval, put a list or picture on the outside of the box.

✻

Costume jewellery is easy to wash, gently, using lukewarm water with a little washing-up liquid and a soft toothbrush.

✻

Silver jewellery benefits from being stored in special jewellery cloth pouches, which prevent tarnishing.

" Style is a magic wand, and turns everything to gold that it touches. "

Logan Pearsall Smith, 1865–1946

Plan ahead

Shopping for special occasion wear is often done in a hurry. Start looking at least six months in advance. Spring and summer styles come in as the January sales are finishing. For autumn and winter styles, start looking as early as July.

Accessorize

Plan even further ahead

You could hire a hat rather than buy one, but
again, start looking at least six months in
advance and book your hat as soon as you
find it. Most hire companies give you a week to
try – and get used to wearing – the hat.

*

❝ *Never run after your own hat – others
will be delighted to do it.* ❞

Unknown

75

" You know it's a bad day when you put your bra on backwards and it fits better. "

Anon.

Underwear

Bra measuring

This is a no-charge service offered by specialist
lingerie shops and most department stores, so
why is it that the majority of women are
wearing the wrong size bra?

Onwards and upwards!

Wearing the correct bra points you in the right direction quite literally and improves your posture. Standing tall creates a confidence that adds style to whatever you're wearing.

A bra wardrobe

Have a choice of bras – an everyday comfy one, a t-shirt bra that gives a smooth appearance, a balconette for empire line necklines, a plunge for special occasions and a strapless for evening. Flesh-coloured bras should be worn with white tops as a white bra can be seen through a white top; a flesh tone is invisible.

Knickers!

Also have a choice of knickers, again, flesh-coloured pants are virtually invisible through light and white garments. Try 'magic' knickers, the modern version of the corset for a tauter tum and smoother hipline.

**" A good deed is like peeing in your pants.
Everyone knows you did it, but only you
can feel it's warmth. "**

Anon

Too hot!

Some say that putting tights and stockings in the freezer before wearing lessens the chances of laddering. Certainly, drying nylon in a tumble dryer or on a radiator weakens the nylon fibre…so try the frozen method!

Take care

If you have long nails, wear rings or have 'gardening' hands, wear special nylon hosiery gloves or cotton gloves when putting on expensive tights or stockings.

Underwear

*" I'll come no more behind your scenes,
David; for the silk stockings and white
bosoms of your actresses excite
my amorous propensities."*

Samuel Johnson, 1709–1784

A good investment

A cheap pair of tights will always let you down.
A good pair will have an extended reinforced
thumb grip area below the waistband, for the
final pull, a higher back waistband that makes
allowance for the bottom, and a leg designed
to correctly fit at the ankle, the knee
and the thigh.

Stop right there!

Use clear nail varnish or soap to stop a ladder in its tracks.

Handy hairdryer

If you're away and you've forgotten some spare underwear, you can always wash it and dry with a hairdryer in minutes. This will work for pants, bras and tights.

❝_Women dress alike all over the world: they dress to be annoying to other women._**❞**

Elsa Schiaparelli, 1896–1973

Shoes, Bags etc.

Gently does it

Stuff damp shoes with newspaper and leave to
dry naturally; never use direct heat.

A refreshing change

Try citrus peel or bicarbonate of soda in shoes
overnight to refresh them.

First impressions

Dirty shoes create a bad impression, so make
sure your shoe cleaning kit contains the colours
you need plus a good suede/nubuck brush.

Try the kitchen cupboard

Patent leather loves petroleum jelly and
furniture polish. Kitchen cream cleanser cleans
scuffed marks on trainers and non-leather
lighter shades.

Safeguard your investments

Always use a special protective spray on pale suede before wearing to build up a protective layer; the same goes for jackets, gloves and handbags. It will lengthen the life and appearance of each item.

To revive suede

If suede looks a little tired, revive it over steam
from the kettle. Small marks can be removed
gently with an emery board.

Anti-ageing

Pale or white shoes and handbags need to be stored in black tissue paper to prevent the light from yellowing them.

Shoes

There are two types of shoes: those that look good and those that are comfortable and easy to wear all day. If you're wearing the look-good ones, pop a comfier pair in your bag for work or driving.

*"If we have not quiet in our minds,
outward comfort will do no more for us
than a golden slipper on a gouty foot."*

John Bunyan, 1628–1688

Waterproof v water repellent

Waterproofing is different to water repellent.
Waterproofing means that the fabric is
completely sealed, nothing can get in or out,
and if a fabric can't breathe then you will get
very hot! Water repellent macs and jackets
have a resistance to water, but a breathability
too – they'll protect you long enough to
find shelter in a downpour!

❝ *I'm an optimist, but an optimist who carries a raincoat.* **❞**

Harold Wilson, 1916–1995

" Sometimes I wish I could go back to the days when I was six and my biggest problem was what kind of dress to put on Barbie..."

Anon.